ØX (3/06 - NEVER)

PowerKids Readers:

The Bilingual Library of the
United States of America™

ILLINOIS

VANESSA BROWN

TRADUCCIÓN AL ESPAÑOL: MARÍA CRISTINA BRUSCA

The Rosen Publishing Group's
PowerKids Press™ & **Editorial Buenas Letras**™
New York

Published in 2005 by The Rosen Publishing Group, Inc.
29 East 21st Street, New York, NY 10010

First Edition

Photo Credits: Cover, pp. 25, 30 (Capitol) © Richard Cummins/Corbis; p. 5 © Joseph Sohm/Visions of America/Corbis; pp. 9, 31 (Farming) © Dwight Ellefsen/SuperStock; p. 11 © Hulton Archive/Getty Images; pp. 13, 30 (Abraham Lincoln) © Library of Congress Prints and Photographs Division; p. 15 © North Wind Picture Archives; pp. 17, 31 (Jane Addams) © Corbis; pp. 19, 30 (Oak) © Richard Hamilton Smith/Corbis; p. 21 © Roger Ressemeyer/Corbis; p. 23 © John Zich/Corbis; pp. 25, 30 (Violet) © Pat O'Hara/Corbis; p. 30 (Fluorite) © José Manuel Sanchis Calvete/Corbis; p. 31 (Frank Lloyd Wright, Ernest Hemingway, Gwendolyn Brooks, Slavery) © Bettmann/Corbis; p. 31 (Ronald Reagan) © Wally McNamee/Corbis; p. 31 (Hilary Rodham Clinton) © Najlah Feanny/Corbis Saba; p. 31 (Bald Eagle) © Eyewire

Library of Congress Cataloging-in-Publication Data

Brown, Vanessa, 1963-
    Illinois / Vanessa Brown ; traducción al español, Cristina Brusca.– 1st ed.
        p. cm. – (The bilingual library of the United States of America)
    Includes index.
    ISBN 1-4042-3140-4 (library binding)
    1. Illinois–Juvenile literature. I. Title. II. Series.

F541.3.B76 2005
977.3–dc22
                                                2004028692

Manufactured in the United States of America

Due to the changing nature of Internet links, Editorial Buenas Letras has developed an online list of Web sites related to the subject of this book. This site is updated regularly. Please use this link to access the list:

http://www.buenasletraslinks.com/ls/illinois

Contents

Contenido

Welcome to Illinois

These are the flag and the seal of the state of Illinois. They both have a bald eagle. The bald eagle stands for America's strength.

Bienvenidos a Illinois

Éstos son la bandera y el escudo de Illinois. En los dos hay un águila calva. El águila calva representa la fuerza de los Estados Unidos de América.

The Flag and State Seal of Illinois

Bandera y escudo de Illinois

Illinois Geography

Illinois borders the states of Missouri, Iowa, Wisconsin, Indiana and Kentucky. The northeast corner of the state is on Lake Michigan.

Geografía de Illinois

Illinois linda con los estados de Misuri, Iowa, Wisconsin, Indiana y Kentucky. En la esquina noreste del estado se encuentra el lago Michigan.

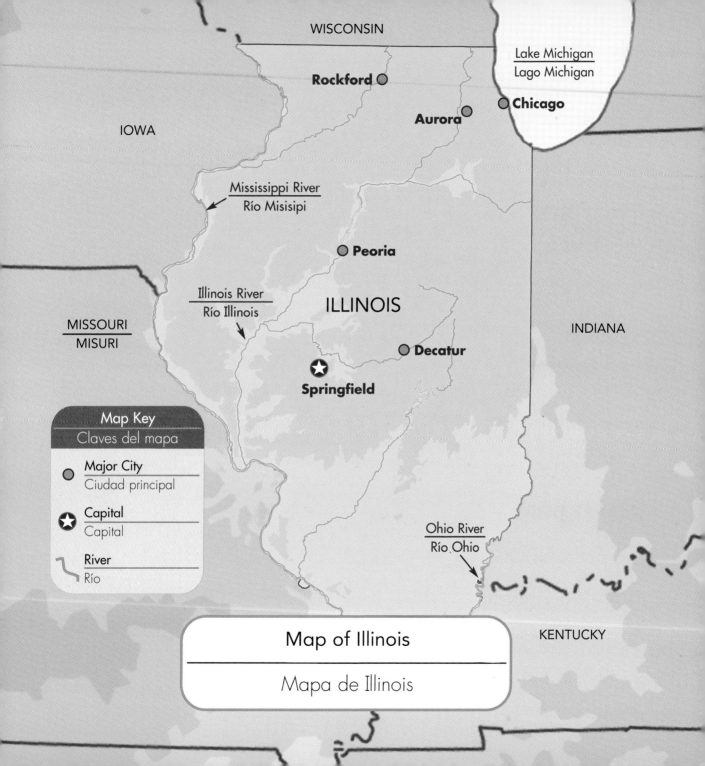

WISCONSIN

Lake Michigan
Lago Michigan

● Rockford

● Aurora

● **Chicago**

IOWA

Mississippi River
Río Misisipi

● Peoria

ILLINOIS

INDIANA

Illinois River
Río Illinois

MISSOURI
MISURI

● Decatur

★ Springfield

Map Key
Claves del mapa

● Major City
Ciudad principal

★ Capital
Capital

〰 River
Río

Ohio River
Río Ohio

KENTUCKY

Map of Illinois

Mapa de Illinois

Illinois has many fields with rich soil. This is very good for farming. Illinois is known as the Prairie State.

Illinois tiene muchos campos de suelo muy rico. Ésta tierra es buena para la agricultura. Illinois es conocido como el Estado Pradera.

The Soil in Illinois is Good for Farming

La tierra en Illinois es buena para sembrar

Illinois History

Illinois gets its name from a Native American group called the Illini or Illiniwek. The name means "strong people." The Illini moved to this area in the year 1500.

Historia de Illinois

Illinois toma su nombre de un grupo de nativos americanos llamado illini o illiniwek. Estos nombres quieren decir "gente fuerte". Los illinis comenzaron a vivir en esta región en el año 1500.

The Illini Meet with European Settlers

Reunión de los illinis con los colonos europeos

Abraham Lincoln was president of the United States from 1861 to 1865. Lincoln fought against slavery and made Illinois his home. Illinois is sometimes known as the Lincoln State.

Abraham Lincoln fue presidente de los Estados Unidos de 1861 a 1865. Lincoln estableció su hogar en Illinois y luchó en contra de la esclavitud. Illinois también es conocido como el Estado de Lincoln.

Abraham Lincoln

In 1871, a big fire started in the city of Chicago. Almost 100,000 people lost their homes. Chicago is the largest city in Illinois.

En 1871 se produjo un gran incendio en la ciudad de Chicago. Entonces, casi 100,000 personas perdieron sus hogares. Hoy día, Chicago es la ciudad más grande de Illinois.

The Chicago Fire on October 8, 1871

El incendio de Chicago, 8 de octubre 1871

Jane Addams worked for a better life for poor people in Illinois. She won the Nobel Peace Prize in 1931. This prize is given to a person who has worked for peace in the world. It is an important honor.

Jane Addams trabajó para mejorar la vida de la gente pobre de Illinois. Addams ganó el Premio Nobel de la Paz en 1931. Este premio se le otorga a la persona que trabaja por la paz del mundo y es un honor muy importante.

Jane Addams

Living in Illinois

Most people in Illinois live in cities. Many other people still live on farms and work in the fields. Farming is important for Illinois.

La vida en Illinois

La mayoría de la gente de Illinois vive en las ciudades. Muchas otras personas viven en granjas y trabajan en el campo. La agricultura es importante para Illinois.

Farmers Working on Illinois Fields

Granjeros trabajando la tierra en Illinois

Chicago is the third-largest city in the United States. In Chicago you can find the tallest building in the United States. It is called the Sears Tower.

Por su tamaño, Chicago es la tercera ciudad de los Estados Unidos. En Chicago puedes encontrar el edificio más alto del país, llamado Torre Sears.

The Sears Tower

La Torre Sears

Illinois Today

Illinois honored the new century with the construction of the Millennium Park in Chicago. The park mixes the beauty of nature with modern buildings.

Illinois, hoy

Illinois celebró el inicio del nuevo siglo con la construcción del Parque del Milenio, en Chicago. Éste parque combina edificios modernos con la belleza de la naturaleza.

A View of the Millennium Park

Una vista del Parque del Milenio

Chicago, Rockford, Peoria, and Aurora are important cities in Illinois. Springfield is the capital of the state of Illinois.

Chicago, Rockford, Peoria y Aurora son importantes ciudades de Illinois. Springfield es la capital del estado de Illinois.

Illinois State Capitol in Spingfield

Capitolio del estado de Illinois, en Springfield

Activity:
Let's Draw the State Flower
The purple violet is Illinois' state flower.

Actividad:
Dibujemos la flor del estado
La violeta es la flor del estado de Illinois.

1

Draw a circle for the center of the flower.

Dibuja un círculo para trazar el centro de la flor.

2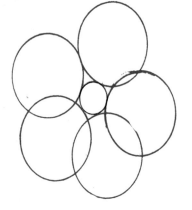

Add five circles around the center. It's okay if the circles overlap.

Agrega cinco círculos alrededor del centro. Los círculos pueden tocarse.

3

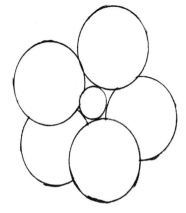

Erase any extra lines.

Borra las líneas
innecesarias

4

Draw straight lines inside
the circles. These circles
are called petals.

Traza líneas rectas dentro
de los círculos. Estos
círculos forman los pétalos.

5

Add shading to your
flower. Your violet is
finished!

Sombrea la flor. ¡Tu
violeta está terminada!

Timeline

Cronología

French explorers Louis Jolliet and Jacques Marquette arrive in Illinois.

1673

Los exploradores franceses Louis Jolliet y Jacques Marquette llegan a Illinois.

Illinois becomes part of the French colony of Louisiana.

1717

Illinois pasa a formar parte de la colonia francesa de Louisiana.

Illinois is ceded to Britain.

1763

Illinois es cedida a Gran Bretaña.

Illinois becomes the twenty-first state.

1818

Illinois se convierte en el estado número veintiuno.

A fire destroys much of the city of Chicago.

1871

Un incendio destruye gran parte de Chicago.

The Sears Tower is finished.

1974

Se termina la Torre Sears.

Jane Byrne becomes the first female mayor of Chicago.

1979

Jane Byrne se convierte en la primera alcaldesa de Chicago.

Carol Moseley-Braun becomes the first African American woman elected to the U.S. Senate.

1992

Carol Moseley-Braun es la primera mujer afroamericana en integrar el senado de E.U.A.

Illinois Events	Eventos en Illinois
January Central Illinois Jazz Festival in Decatur	Enero Festival de jazz de Central Illinois, en Decatur
February Winter Carnival in Galena	Febrero Carnaval blanco, en Galena
March St. Patrick's Day Parade in Chicago	Marzo Desfile del día de San Patricio, en Chicago
May Old Capitol Art Fair in Springfield	Mayo Feria de arte del antiguo capitolio, en Springfield
June–July Taste of Chicago at Grant Park in Chicago	Junio-julio Taste of Chicago en el Parque Grant, en Chicago
September Chicago Jazz Festival Apple Festival in Long Grove	Septiembre Festival de jazz de Chicago Festival de la manzana, en Long Grove
November International Folk Fair in Chicago	Noviembre Feria internacional del folclore, en Chicago
November–January Lake Shelbyville Festival of Lights	Noviembre-enero Festival de las luces Lake Shelbyville

Illinois Facts/Datos sobre Illinois

<u>Population</u>
12 million

<u>Población</u>
12 millones

<u>Capital</u>
Springfield

<u>Capital</u>
Springfield

<u>State Motto</u>
State sovereignty,
national union

<u>Lema del estado</u>
Soberanía del estado,
unión nacional

<u>State Flower</u>
Purple Violet

<u>Flor del estado</u>
Violeta

<u>State Bird</u>
Cardinal

<u>Ave del estado</u>
Cardenal

<u>State Nickname</u>
The Prairie State,
The Lincoln State

<u>Mote del estado</u>
Estado Pradera
Estado de Lincoln

<u>State Tree</u>
White Oak

<u>Árbol del estado</u>
Roble blanco

<u>State Song</u>
"Illinois"

<u>Canción del estado</u>
"Illinois"

<u>State Gemstone</u>
Fluorite

<u>Piedra preciosa</u>
Fluorita

Famous Illinoisans/Illinoisanos famosos

Frank Lloyd Wright
(1869–1959)

Architect
Arquitecto

Jane Addams
(1880–1935)

Nobel prize winner
Premio Nobel de la Paz

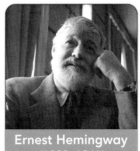

Ernest Hemingway
(1899–1961)

Author
Autor

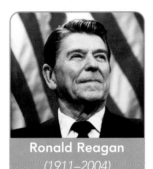

Ronald Reagan
(1911–2004)

U.S. President
Presidente de E.U.A

Gwendolyn Brooks
(1917–)

Poet
Poeta

Hilary R. Clinton
(1947–)

U.S. Senator
Senadora de E.U.A.

Words to Know/Palabras que debes saber

bald eagle
águila calva

border
frontera

farming
agricultura

slavery
esclavitud

Here are more books to read about Illinois:
Otros libros que puedes leer sobre Illinois:

In English/En inglés:
Illinois
By Somervill, Barbara A.
Children's Press, 2001

In Spanish/En español:
Illinois, el estado pradera
por Feeley, Kathleen
World Almanac Library, 2004

Words in English: 282   Palabras en español: 310

Index

Índice